# HAPPY BIRTHDAY
# PLANET EARTH

## The Instant of Co-Operation

*The whole of Creation*
*is now giving birth*
*to a universal species,*
*forecast in the example of Jesus,*
*matured in the experience*
*of Earthbound, infant humanity,*
*and soon to be embodied*
*in all those*
*who consciously work together*
*to restore the Earth,*
*to serve existing lifekind,*
*and to impregnate the universe*
*with new life.*

## BARBARA MARX HUBBARD

*Ocean Tree Books*
Santa Fe

*Also by Barbara Marx Hubbard:*

*The Hunger of Eve:*
*A Woman's Odyssey Toward the Future*

*The Evolutionary Journey*

*The Book of Co-Creation:*
*An Evolutionary Interpretation of the New Testament (forthcoming)*

OCEAN TREE BOOKS
Post Office Box 1295
Santa Fe, New Mexico 87504
*Ask for our catalog of enduring books that touch the spirit.*

For information about tapes on Co-Creation write
Highlight Productions, 6124 Fairway Dr., Cincinnatti, Ohio 45212
and New Visions, P.O. Box 5102, Gainesville, Florida 32602

International Standard Book Number: 0-943734-08-8

Library of Congress Catalog Card Number: 86-62081

*This book is dedicated to
the Instant of Co-Operation*

*—a moment close at hand—*

*after which
we shall no longer sleep
but be transformed
from children of Adam
to children of God.*

# Contents

# How this Book Originated

I was the mother of five children, an agnostic in my religious beliefs, yet also I had a lifelong hunger for something more, for a purpose beyond the satisfactions of ordinary living. In those earlier years, I had no idea what was going to occur in my life—two very unpredictable surprises.

One day in February 1966 I had what I would call an expanded reality experience: it was a pre-cognition of a *planetary event* to come which would change the world forever. I had been reading Reinhold Niebuhr on community; he quoted St. Paul's phrase: *All men are members of one body.*

As I walked upon the hill that freezing cold day, I was thinking about the story of the birth of Christ, although I had been an agnostic most of my life. A child was born and the world was changed forever. *One* story that everyone could understand. Ours must also be one story, for we are of one planet. So I asked the universe a silent question: What is *our* story? What in our age is comparable to the birth of Christ? What is happening on Earth now?

At that moment, my mind's eye penetrated the blue cocoon of Earth. I was in the blackness of outer space, witnessing our planet as a living organism in the throes of its struggle to become one body. I realized I was a cell in that body. "We" were struggling to breathe. The pain of starvation coursed through "our" body. The mass media (our infantile nervous system) carried the "news" of the pain to one and all. We were bursting the limits of Earth as our population grew. For one instant, I felt the pain of the whole body. Then, suddenly, we reached together beyond ourselves, attracted by a point of focus beyond the planet, as during the first lunar landing.

With that shared point of attention, a sudden shift occurred. Empathy began to flood the consciousness of all people. An irresistible attraction drew us together. People gathered spontaneously throughout the world. A new, common tone was heard—a single vibration coursing through the planet. With one accord, we experienced ourselves as one body. We opened our collective eyes and saw the Earth bathed in intelligent light which was about to communicate with us all. And *we* were about to speak with *it*. Our joy permeated the whole world. We smiled together— *'a planetary smile!'*

And in my vision, we were about to make direct contact with the Light itself, when the "movie" shut down and the technicolor faded away.

I was alone on the hill in Lakeville, Connecticut, with tears freezing to my cheeks. Then I heard the words: "Our story is a birth. It is the birth of mankind. What the saints and seers of the human race predicted is true. We are one body, born into this universe. We are to be immortal. We have seen through a glass darkly, and now we are seeing face to face...*Go tell the story of our birth.*"

I ran home, home to my husband and children, and told them I must tell the story of the birth of mankind. And I began my life as a "futurist," telling the story of the nature of what is coming—of what all our struggle and preparation and expectation has been for.

Then in 1980, I again had a profound experience, this time with a "presence" of Christ. This happened at Mt. Calvary Monastery near Santa Barbara. Again it was February. I was taking a ride with my sister to the Botanical Gardens, when I saw a little sign that read, 'Mt. Calvary'. Suddenly I felt an urgent compulsion to go there—*now.* As we turned up the steep, winding road, an electric excitement brought tears to my eyes. I felt a "light field" surrounding me. "Something is going to happen to me," I told my sister, who was staring at me in surprise. At the top of the hill was a little Episcopal monastery. Above it in the sky were hang-gliders, their pilots floating in weightless ecstasy.

Quite unexpectedly, this Christ "presence" turned to me. It was the same feeling as the light that bathed the Earth in the earlier planetary birth experience. Clearly and directly, I heard the words:

My resurrection was real. It was a forecast of your own when you learn to love God above all else, your neighbor as yourself, and yourself as Me, a natural Christ. That great commandment of pure love, combined with the knowledge of God's processes of creation gained by science in the last 2000 years, is the formula for victory.

It is your own maturing which is the key. Take the perspective of a more mature species, what it will be like when the human race grows up, stops fighting and starts using its full capacities harmoniously. As each person has a higher, wiser self, so does the species-as-a-whole.

*Be* members of a more mature species. *You have the power of a natural Christ.* This is what I came to Earth to reveal. You can do what I did and even greater works shall you do.

Stop being children! Start being like me. Yours are the power, yours the glory, yours the triumph if you align your will with the will of God, and love your neighbor as yourself.

You—all of you who are desirous and ready—are the way. Be a beacon of light unto yourselves. This tiny band, this brave congregation of souls attracted to the future of the world, are my avant garde, my new order of the future.

They are self-selected souls who have come to Earth to carry the miracle of the resurrection into action as the transformation of *Homo Sapiens* to *Homo universalis*.

The words came with a rhythm of their own, faster than I could remember them. I took out my journal and began to write at lightning speed as the monks of the Order of the Holy Cross walked by, smiling pleasantly. I wondered what they'd think of all this. Is it blasphemous to believe in the reality of the promise?

I entered the monastery as a guest, for a silent retreat. I was lovingly guided to look at the predictive passages of the New Testament, which I had never read. The scriptures opened the floodgates of my mind. The voice of Christ seemed to guide my hand. As I read I wrote, and what was revealed to me I recorded in a document that parallels the New Testament, verse by verse—it is called *The Book of Co-Creation.* The key message in it is that *the alternative to Armageddon is a planetary pentecost: when a critical mass of humanity is gathered in consciousness in the place of one accord.*

## The Instant of Co-Operation

The presence guiding my hand called it the great "World Instant of Co-Operation." It described the rapid empowerment of all who are joined in consciousness: Each person who is attracted to this field experiences a profound sense of anticipation and empathy for others. At a certain point this empathy becomes exponential, doubling the number of people attracted very quickly—possibly even every few minutes. People on the street, in shops, in homes and hospitals, in schools and cars and airplanes, in conferences, in the halls of government, industry, labor and academia—great numbers will suddenly feel and know that something profound is happening worldwide.

Perhaps it is like this: When atoms are aligned in the same direction on the physical plane (following physical laws) magnetism occurs. Similarly, when thoughts come aligned on the mental plane, a kind of psychomagnetism, a certain one-mindedness, occurs—and the understanding between people is immediate. It's something like what the English biologist Rupert Sheldrake calls the Morphogenetic Field, an energy around the planet connecting everything; when the field gets "saturated" with something new, change occurs rapidly everywhere.

At some point, and in one instant, a critical mass of humanity *experiences* that we are one body, we are universal, we are being born. We open our collective eyes...and we see face to face what we have seen through a glass darkly.

And then I heard:

> And I will be enabled to contact all of you at once. This is my dream, this is my passion, this is my desire—to have all of you paying attention to me at once through the activation of your own inner experience of your potential to be me, rather than relying on priests, mystics, or saints, beloved though they are. Their work is done. Yours has begun.
>
> As the planetary smile ripples through the nervous systems of Earth, and the instant of co-operation begins, and empathy floods the feelings of the whole body of Earth, separation is

overcome, and I appear to all of you at once. I appear to you from within as a voice, and as a vision of yourself as an evolving being...

For remember, the promise I made is of a personal future in a transformed body. This means you will also have what I have now. I am real. I am tangible. I am alive. I can speak to each of you through your inner ear if you will listen. I can appear to each of you through your inner eye if you will look.

At the moment of contact, I will appear to you both through inner experience and through external communication on the nervous system of the world.

You will all feel, hear and see my presence at one instant in time.

The silence in heaven will conclude in peace. The fateful destruction will be avoided. The planetary celebration will begin for the birth of humankind in the universe, a blessed cosmic child eagerly awaited by the evolved beings through the universe without end. Hallelujah! Amen!

*    *    *

My human speculation is that the Instant of Co-Operation will be a shared experience of a *loving Presence*, and the realization that we are neither individually nor collectively alone in this universe. Many in the Judeo-Christian world have personally experienced this loving Presence as the Christ. They have anticipated a "second coming" which has yet to occur. Other cultures have shared the loving Presence differently, and accordingly they have slightly different personifications and expectations of its fulfillment.

None has ever been known precisely when and how the loving Presence will express its fulfillment. As Jesus said, "only the Father knows." But our expectation of fulfillment, in all the forms it takes, reflects an accurate racial knowledge: evolution does not proceed only by incremental steps, but also by quantum leaps in the fullness of time—timing which many may intuit but none can know with certainty.

Many believe that the "fullness of time" for such an evolutionary quantum leap is close at hand. Enough of us are now aligned mentally in a "psychomagnetic field of attraction" that we are set to receive together globally what has formerly been experienced only by isolated individuals and small groups. As the 'vertical' alignment to God is experienced by a critical mass of individuals, 'horizontal' alignment unites God's human family.

The Instant of Co-Operation is nothing less than a *planetary pentecost*. When enough of us—a quantity we are approaching—share the co-operative vision, spirit will pour through all and any who are paying attention. We will all hear from within the same voice, in our own language, speak of the mighty works of humanity at one with God. The illusion of separateness will be over. This experience will alter forever the planetary state of mind and our perception of the nature of reality.

## To the Second Generation of Disciples:

Almost two thousand years ago, a small band of people believed in the reality of the life, death and resurrection of the Christ Jesus. They preached that we must prepare ourselves spiritually, for the "kingdom of heaven was at hand." They believed the promises that the Christ had made:

> *Verily, verily, I say unto you, he that believeth on me hath everlasting life.* (John 6:47)

> *He who believes in me, will also do the works that I do; and greater works than these will he do; because I go to the Father.* (John 14:12)

The first disciples formed churches to retain and nourish this extraordinary promise of a new humanity, that would be capable—as Jesus was—of transcending the limits of the creature-human condition.

Like the first disciples, many who are now at the threshold of the second millenium also believe in the reality of such transformation. We sense that out of our current crises are also emerging new spiritual, social and scientific potentials. We further sense that if we use these potentials in a harmonious alignment with the Will of God, we can activate both the individual and collective capacities to transcend self-centered consciousness, 'planet-boundedness,' scarcity, warfare, mental/physical disease, bodily degeneration and even death itself. We see our possibility of acting out the Christ's promise of becoming *fully* human beings, eternally evolving in a universe of many mansions, consciously cooperating with the ongoing process of universal creation.

*Happy Birth Day Planet Earth* contains the first published excerpts from *The Book of Co-Creation: An Evolutionary Interpretation of the New Testament.* It tells the key elements of the new story, in present moment concepts, of the fulfillment of the promises Jesus made and early Christians had a glimmering of long ago.

There is an interesting timeliness in its publication, for in 1986 and the time just ahead, several major global events are planned which actually have the quality spoken of in *The Book of Co-Creation* that could bring about a world of co-operation—events which have the potential to align the consciousness of a "critical mass" of humanity in an experience of shared spirit.

We have witnessed, or been a part of, germinal global events and widespread linkages of spirit already (the *'We Are the World'* themes of *Live Aid, Band Aid* and *Hands Across America*). As this edition goes to press, there are two events scheduled for December 31, 1986, which have the possibility of bringing together two billion people or more in the spirit of cooperation via global television. These are *The First Earth Run,* and the Planetary Commission's *World Healing Meditation.*

Using a flaming torch as the visual symbol embodying the spirit of cooperation, thousands of runners from different nations are expected to circle the world during a four month period. They will arrive at the UN in New York at midnight GMT on December 31, 1986, at the formal closing of the International Year of Peace. At the moment the runners light an eternal flame at the UN, two billion people may light candles around the globe.

"The spiritual purpose of The First Earth Run," according to planner David Gershon, "is to create an event of such magnitude that we are compelled by the image it generates—a great thread of light passed around the world by tens of thousands of people, linking us and showing us that we are together—igniting a global sense of hope for the future."

The Planetary Commission's event calls for 50 million people to meditate and to pray at noon GMT the same day, December 31. This is approximately one percent of the entire human race.

"Our objective is obvious," writes John Randolph Price, author of *The Planetary Commission.* "Why not reverse the polarity of the (mental) force field and achieve a critical mass of positive energy? Why not insure a chain reaction of self-sustaining good around and through this planet? If these many men and women would meditate simultaneously and release their energies into the earth's magnetic field, the entire vibration of the planet would begin to change."

The late futurist R. Buckminster Fuller called for "the shift from weaponry to livingry" in the present decade. In every field, nation and discipline there are now mounting numbers of men and women, often unknown to one another, who are actually designing the framework for a New Order of the Ages. The preparations have begun and the process is accelerating. And once the field of consciousness of the world has shifted from fear to love, the human race will be empowered to build a global society in which all people are truly free to do their best, yet are consciously united as one magnificent universal Being. We will be reconnected to each other, to nature and to God. The separation will be over. The former things will have passed away.

This vision has its roots in the Judeo-Christian tradition. There are other versions of how we will fulfill our transcendent dream. Yet all visions of the future of the world's great cultures converge in the expectation of humanity at one with nature and with God. Now is the time for all of us to consciously fulfill the dream of the ages.

Barbara Marx Hubbard
January 1986

# 1
# Avoiding Planetary Abortion

*II TIMOTHY 1*

¹³ *Hold fast the form of sound words, which thou hast heard of me, in faith and love which is in Christ Jesus.*

¹⁴ *That good thing which was committed unto thee keep by the Holy Ghost which dwelleth in us.*

Can you believe that the thought you choose to hold in your mind creates reality? Can you believe that if you 'hold fast the form of sound words' they will become manifest in your life and in the life of the world?

It is so.

Think carefully. Think clearly. Think aspirationally. Focus upon your vision of what you want to become. Ask your inner calling to speak to you. Let the compass of joy guide your thoughts till they focus on the magnetic attraction for a creative act in the world.

What are you born to do? Image yourself doing your heart's desire. Conceive yourself doing everything you ever dreamed of doing, being everything you ever dreamed of being.

Place that vision in the context of the evolution of humankind toward *full* humanity. See yourself participating in that evolution, joining with all others also responding to a unique call from within.

Connect with them. Take communion with them in your mind's eye. Fuse with them in the body of light in the cocoon of transformation. (See message entitled "Focus.")

Wherever two or three are gathered in my name, there is the church. You are in church when you do as I do . . . and even more. Church is not a building. It is a body of acts leading toward humankind as one living body of infinite diversity born into the universe of infinite light and life.

Keep your vision clear by the power of "the Holy Ghost which dwelleth in us." The Holy Ghost is your connection to the designing intelligence of the universe. It is in every person. It is alive with a life more vital than flesh and blood can know. It is available to you at all times. All that is required is that you call upon it.

*Evolution proceeds by choice, not by chance, from this stage onward.*

You arrived at the stage of *Homo sapiens* by unconscious biological selection, a highly sophisticated process of development that works without the knowing participation of the organisms involved. You will now proceed to the stage of *Homo universalis* by conscious individual selection. Each person has a chance to make a choice.

The choice is: do you wish to become a natural Christ, a universal human, or do you wish to die?

To become a universal human you must:

- Love God above all else;
- Love yourself and your neighbor as a natural Christ;
- Visualize yourself as a natural Christ—the next stage of your evolution.

Practice every minute of the day Christ-centeredness:

- Thinking the thoughts of Christ;
- Seeing the world as he sees it;
- Loving each other as he loved you.

Practice Christ-abilities:

- You can heal as he healed.
- You can create abundance as he did with the loaves and the fishes.

16

- You can communicate by direct thoughts.
- You can know and do the will of our Father, the God-force, the pattern in the process of evolution.
- You can evolve your body from perishable to imperishable by signaling your body you are ready to rejuvenate, purifying your thoughts from all negativity, creating an inner environment of deep peace, absolute faith, incessant prayer and unshakable joy.
- You can leave this Earth alive.
- You can send signals of thought into the universe alerting your brothers and sisters that you are born from the womb of Earth and are ready to communicate with them.

All this you potentially can do now. More, much more shall you soon do. Now you see through a glass darkly, moving as a child in the night. Then you shall *see* face to face, *acting* as a young co-creator, a joint-heir with Christ.

Christ-consciousness and Christ-abilities are the natural inheritance of every human being now on Earth. When the word of this hope has reached all the nations, the end of this phase of evolution shall come. All will know their choice. All will be required to choose.

There will be mighty dislocations and magnificent relocations. All who choose to be natural Christs will be guided from within as to how to proceed. All who choose not to evolve will die off; their souls will begin again within a different planetary system which will serve as kindergarten for the transition from self-centered to whole-centered being.

The kindergarten class of Earth will be over. Humankind's collective power is too great to be inherited by self-centered, infantile people. Nuclear bombs, biospheric collapse, the destruction of life itself is the power that has been given you through the maturation of the intellect and its servants, science and technology.

This power cannot be taken away. It can only be used or misused. Its use is to restore the Earth, to free all people from want, and to impregnate the universe with the seed of Earth, with new life, new co-creators—the sons and daughters of man, the heirs of God. Continued misuse of your powers will abort the planetary life cycle at the moment of birth. Yours will be a still-born planet, murdered by the lack of awareness of who you are.

17

Your self-image, your sense of identity, is the key, dearly beloveds. Those of you who see yourselves as natural Christs will evolve. Those who see yourselves as natural victims of forces beyond your control will be victimized.

*As you see yourself, so shall you be.*

Artists of the world, you are needed now to envision humanity emerging from its womb of self-centeredness into its universal phase. Every great age created a new image of man. Yours is still a blank. You see with the inner eye, yet when you open your outer eye, you do not see yourselves as co-creators. On television, in the films, in the newspapers, you see yourselves as victims and destroyers more often than as powerful creators. This self-image will be fatal if it is not soon changed.

Artists of the world: Envision! Art is the interface between the inner and outer vision. It is imagination made visible.

You have been given the word. You have been told the act. You have not yet been given the visual image of ourselves as universal, imperishable Christ-like beings.

What will you look like then . . . when you see face to face, not through a glass darkly? You shall see each other as thoughts, not as things. Every thought you are thinking will be instantly visible to another. Nothing will be hidden. That is what it means to see face to face.

Now your bodies hide your thoughts from each other. You can walk into a room thinking 'I hate you' while smiling, and hide your thought with that smile. At your next stage, your thought will be apparent. Your telepathy will be like television: clear, obvious images of your state of being will be immediately picked up by the mind of another person. You will be totally revealed.

Your intentions will also be manifest immediately. Energy follows thought. What you think, you will create, as Jesus did—from food to a new body. The powers of materialization will be yours. You will attract energy around the nucleus of a thought and produce a thing.

This is why *only* natural Christs can survive into the next stage of evolution. It is not only the external powers of nuclear bombs that can be misused. Far more terrible would be the misuse of thought. To think a hateful thought would be to destroy the hated person. To think a jealous thought would be to annihilate your love. To think a covetous thought would be to appropriate the wealth.

To allow self-centered humans to enter the next stage of evolution would be like giving a two-year-old child the powers of a psychic surgeon, a genetic engineer, and a Chief of Staff of the nuclear forces of the world!

Just as any cell, once cancerous, can infect the whole body with destructive growth, every human in the body of humanity can destroy the whole after a certain stage of power has been collectively attained.

Even now one person can build and explode a nuclear bomb. One person can destroy the water supply of a whole city. One person can hijack a jumbo jet and hold a nation at ransom. Such risks are the price you pay for inheriting the powers of the Creator.

In such circumstances, only the good can evolve. Since the powers of co-creation are also powers of co-destruction, there is a built-in limit to selfishness just as there is with the cancerous cell. If either succeeds, it surely fails, killing the whole system that sustains it. If one person in a state of selfishness were to inherit the powers of a natural Christ, he could destroy the universe.

This cannot be.

This will not be—it is against unbreakable law.

Therefore, dearly beloveds, 'hold fast the form of sound words.' Think only the thoughts you think with me.

# 2

# Prepare to See Together

*I PETER 4*

<sup></sup>⁷ *But the end of all things is at hand: be ye therefore sober, and watch unto prayer.*

The quantum instant of transformation is at hand. Therefore, be sober; that is, be sensitive and aware to what is happening both around you and within you.

Around you, confusion will increase. Within you, focus will sharpen, until you are like a laser beam of coherent light in the dark forest of the night.

Shine with coherence. Be a beacon of light unto yourselves, all those called to enter the New Order of the Future. Do these things which I ask, then more shall you do.

If you do not do these things, then *less* shall you do—ever less until finally, at the last trumpet, you do nothing at all. You will be immobilized by the transformation, which you cannot understand because you have not prepared while you had the time.

\* \* \*

*PHILIPPIANS 3*

²⁰ *For our conversation is in heaven . . .*

Those who have spent life times of training in personal transformation are everywhere among you, setting high examples of capability for those in whom the flame of expectation burns.

What is the flame expecting? It is expecting union with God through self-evolution, personal and planetary. It is expecting union with God by maturing sufficiently to know him.

A single cell cannot know a whole body, yet it has the design of the whole body in its nucleus. A single person cannot know the whole design of Creation, yet each of you has the design in your consciousness.

Single cells, when united, create eyes to see both the single cells and the whole body. It is the whole which forms the organ to see the parts, not the parts which see the whole. It is the whole which sees itself.

Single individuals, when united into an inter-communicating planetary body, will have eyes to see each person as part of the whole that is greater than the sum of its parts. Single individuals, bonded for an instant by sharing awareness of the intention of Creation, will know the whole *and* its parts.

It is through your unity that you will know the next phase of God's design and your individual parts in it. The phase of personal salvation is concluding. The phase of collective conscious evolution is beginning.

The purpose of this text is to create sufficient unity among those whose memory of the future is awakening so that together they may have eyes to see and ears to hear what none of them could see or hear alone.

To penetrate beyond the quantum instant, to see beyond the present crisis to the transformed world, you must unite, dearly beloveds, you must unite—not organizationally, but spiritually. Combine your flames and intuitions until you see that which is greater than the sum of your parts, and then do that which none can do alone.

# 3

# The Selection Process

What is 'evil'?  What is 'the devil'?

Evil—the devil—is evolution's selection process that constantly weeds out the weaker from the stronger.  It is the steady pressure of the forces of destruction, dis-integration, dissent, decay, devolution and death which test every body every instant of every day for weakness.  When its pressure penetrates to a weak spot, it corrodes with the almighty force of God, destroying that which cannot endure to evolve.

Evil comes in many guises.  The selection mechanism of evolution is highly intelligent, for its function is to uncover and destroy everything that cannot inherit the kingdom of heaven, everything that would prevent the kingdom of heaven from being fulfilled on Earth.

Selfishness, hostility, fear, anxiety are all characteristics which must be selected against at this stage of evolution. Only those who develop a sensitivity to the patterns in the evolutionary process (or the will of God) will be capable of attaining the next stage.

The intention of the Creator is that all creatures come to know him. Humanity, as the growing tip of nature on planet Earth, is to know him consciously, to become ever more like him. Those characteristics in human beings which prevent them from knowing God, from becoming more God-like, from sensing their relationship to the whole—will be weeded out.

God's will is for all life to inherit the kingdom. His will is for all creatures to become co-creative. God's intelligence operates everywhere. His method of transformation is known as evolution. It has operated before life began and it will continue to operate in the post-biological phase, when *conscious* evolution prevails.

God's selection mechanism is experienced as evil by those who are resisting it. The forces of 'good' are in constant interaction with the forces of 'evil.' That which can evolve is always contending with that which would prevent it from evolving.

Every hurdle to your own growth is God's selection mechanism at work, dearly beloveds. It is a necessary test to give you the opportunity to qualify. If you respond to the hurdle by leaping over it, by keeping your eye on the 'kingdom,' you will pass the test. If you respond by fear and failure to leap, you will be given chance after chance—forgiven, forgiven, forgiven—but only until the time of the quantum transformation, when one phase of evolution is over and another is to begin.

Then you have no more chances. Incremental changes cease. All those humans capable of cooperating to self-transcend will do so. All those elements remaining in a state of self-centeredness, maintaining the illusion of separation, will become extinct.

The forces of 'evil' will have done their task. 'Satan' will be buried forever, for this stage. Self-consciousness will be a subsystem of wholistic consciousness. The 'devil's' work on *Homo sapiens* will be complete. Only that spectrum of human consciousness freely able to attune to the whole and hear the inner voice for God will survive.

Just as Cro-Magnon and Neanderthal humans became extinct, so will selfish humans. This is necessary, for their temperament is not viable. The selfish cannot inherit the powers of co-creation, which in their state of consciousness would amount to powers of self-destruction.

If the selfish were to inherit the evolutionary capacities (early external aspects of Christ-ability)—nuclear energy, bio-technology, longevity, self-replicating machines, the power to build new worlds, etc.—they would self-destruct, and in the process destroy the whole.

Why do the selfish exist at all? Why are not all children of God ready to graduate to heirs of God? The answer is freedom. We are endowed by our Creator with one basic inalienable right: the freedom to follow the will of God, or to ignore it and become extinct.

Thy kingdom *will* come. Thy will *will* be done. Nothing that is unwilling to do the will of God can survive. Such is the design of creation.

The will of God is pure goodness, pure love, pure power. It can only be inherited by those who freely choose it. This was the Godly decision: to grant intelligent life the freedom to become co-creative with him, or to choose extinction.

The design is irresistible. God's will will be done. You have the choice of freely attuning to it so that your will and God's will are one, or of freely choosing not to attune, not to love God above all else and your neighbor as yourself.

The latter choice is your ticket to extinction. The tribulations will increase and the selection process ('evil' forces) will discriminate with ever greater refinement, until a final selection is made in this stage of Earth's evolution. Jesus told you to be prepared at all times, for you know not when the quantum instant will come.

> *But as the days of Noah were, so shall also the coming of the Son of man be.*
>
> *For as in the days that were before the flood they were eating and drinking, marrying and giving in marriage, until the day that Noah entered into the ark,*
>
> *And knew not until the flood came, and took them all away; so shall also the coming of the Son of man be.*
>
> *Then shall two be in the field; the one shall be taken, and the other left.*
>
> *Two women shall be grinding at the mill; the one shall be taken, and the other left.*

*Watch therefore: for ye know not what hour your Lord doth come. (Matthew 24:37-42)*

At one moment, all appears tranquil. In the next instant, all hell breaks loose. Suddenly, all is new.

The selection process is not crude, but extremely refined, carefully weeding out among seemingly identical beings. How? By identifying and 'saving' those who have become resistant to 'evil,' those strains of human temperament who have withstood the diseases of the modern age—fear, hostility, guilt, alienation—by becoming centered in the 'holy place' within each person wherein the higher self—the Holy Spirit, the voice for God—speaks constantly, lovingly to all people.

How would the whole system select among its parts for those members capable of attuning to the whole? By a system of communication. In a cellular body the DNA communicates the plan through a 'messenger' RNA, who gets the 'template' or pattern—and goes forth among the macro-molecules to attract those capable of identifying with (become identical with) the pattern carried by the RNA. The attracted molecules are drawn into the cell and are given complex instructions to perform highly specific functions within the cell. They self-transcend, not by leaping from molecule-hood to cell-hood, but by integration with other macro-molecules in a new pattern which is greater than the sum of its parts. They transcend by synergistic cooperation.

Within an embryonic organism, cells at first are multi-purpose and omniscient. Each cell carries the entire design for building the whole body; cloning a body from a single cell is, therefore, possible. However, at a certain point in embryonic development, differentiation occurs. Each cell is signaled to perform a specialized organic task in cooperation with millions of other cells also signaled to a specific function. Thus all cells building eyes have a common but unique task. As cells serve to differentiate the whole body into ears, heart, brain, lungs, and other parts, they receive communication of exquisite refinement down to the tiniest detail.

In a diseased or defective embryo some of the cells make an error in following the design, the 'will' of the DNA. The consequence for not following the genetic design is death of the whole embryo and all its parts.

25

If the gestating organism is 95 percent perfect—that is 'normal'—yet its heart valve doesn't work, or its little lungs don't expand, or it gets tangled in its umbilical life-support system while making the transition down the birth canal, the whole organism dies. Little defects may pass through the final judgment on the work of the cells within the womb. But major defects will cause the process to abort, and the organism to die.

From the organism's point of view, 'evil' has been done. From the point of view of the social body, 'evil' has been prevented from contaminating the larger whole.

Within a social body, human society and all life on planet Earth, some process of communication from the parts to the whole must also exist. We only recently discovered the mechanism of DNA—how the body-building plan is communicated. We are still exploring how trillions of cells 'know' how to build a living body in the womb, to go through the 'cataclysm' of birth into a new environment, and then proceed to turn on their womb-built systems to operate in a seemingly hostile world.

It is therefore to be expected that we will also discover how the God force communicates its design to individual humans who are all members of one body.

Is it telepathically, by an inner voice? Is the 'Holy Spirit,' which has been described and experienced by religious sensitives from time immemorial, God's communication system to members of a social body? Is the key characteristic for which we will be selected at the cosmic birth the capacity to listen and act upon an inner communication signal from the Creator?

Those who are practicing the development of inner listening through prayer and meditation of all kinds (whether deliberately or not does not matter) are building 'sound studios' to pick up the signal of God. They are clearing 'static' from their system, perfecting their tuning capabilities and learning to distinguish the pure inner voice from the noisy, whimsical whine of the personality.

When the disorder increases, the signals will intensify. All members of the social body who are 'listening' will know what to do. Those not listening will be confused, "one shall be taken, the other left."

'Evil' will appear to destroy—and indeed it will. It will destroy all those who cannot attune to the design at its coming stage, for life is future-oriented. Nature is less concerned about individual survival, than with the evolution of the whole to ever higher degrees of freedom, union and consciousness of God.

The discovery of God's communication system will probably be made by those in closest communication with him—those whose nervous systems and brains and intentions are so developed as to be attracted to enlightenment and love.

The humans who can best survive the tribulations will be those whose intuition is best attuned to the evolutionary design, and whose intellect is best able to carry out the intentions picked up through attunement to the larger whole system.

\* \* \*

Each of you is now, at this very instant, receiving signals—if you have eyes to see and ears to hear. Listen carefully, dearly beloveds. Learn to focus your attention continually on the 'still small voice' within each of you. 'Be still, listen, and know that I am God.'

- Strengthen the magnetic needle of your attention by faith in the process of creation. Faith is a magnet that attracts the signals.
- Pray constantly for guidance. Prayer is the telepathic signal from the part to the whole, attracting its attention to your readiness to do more.
- Refuse to believe that the appearance of the existing world is the ultimate nature of reality. Refuse to accept the *status quo* as the way things are. Things are in the process of change, dearly beloveds. Invisible processes are at work giving birth to a whole world. The whole Creation suffers and groans—and has been so suffering for thousands of years, awaiting the time when the whole planetary system would develop human beings who are conscious enough to become co-creative with God's design.
- Reject all existing ideologies and belief systems that would limit you to your present incomplete stage of development. Reject all counsel to stay as you are. Ask that you become *all* that you are: a natural Christ.
- Let the flame of expectation in you burn to a fire and light your enthusiasm, till the love of God fills your whole being.

- Surrender yourself to the design of creation by carving out a still place within you to listen for the voice of God.
- Make direct contact. Let the electricity of God's communication system transfigure you as Jesus was transfigured after he was recognized by Peter: "Thou art the Christ, the son of the living God."

From the time of that act of recognition Jesus accepted his fateful role. He told his disciples how he must go into Jerusalem, suffer, be killed and be raised on the third day. Then he brought them up into a high mountain:

> *And was transfigured before them: and his face did shine as the sun, and his raiment was white as the light.*
>
> *. . . a bright cloud overshadowed them: and behold a voice out of the cloud, which said, This is my beloved Son, in whom I am well pleased; hear ye him. (Matthew 17:2,5)*

For each of you, the process is the same:

First you must be recognized as the son of God by your lower self, your animal-human body/mind, who has experienced you as a mortal organism born to live, age and die. The lower self must be infused with enough light to see beyond the five senses. The recognition by your lower self that you are a son of God will free you to transform.

Next you will 'go to Jerusalem.' You will resolutely decide to die to this ego-centered stage of evolution (be crucified) and arise as a new being, a natural Christ—which is every human's inheritance as a natural heir of God.

Your lower self will protest. You must teach your lower self lovingly, as Jesus did his disciples, that a far greater victory is to be gained by your transformation than by maintenance of the existing human condition.

You will clear your system of all negativity and guard your thoughts with a sword of steel. The natural process of self-evolution will occur. You will triumph. All elements of your being will align themselves with your highest intention.

Then you will be transfigured. You will shine with light. You will know your identity as a son of God. You will be among the

28

self-elect. When the tribulations come you will hear the voice, the trumpet shall sound, and you shall be gathered together with the self-elect from all over the world.

Then shall the selection be made for this phase of evolution.

*And he shall set the sheep on his right hand, but the goats on the left.*

*Then shall the King say unto them on his right hand, Come, ye blessed of my Father, inherit the kingdom prepared for you from the foundation of the world. (Matthew 25:33,34)*

Those who have freely elected to listen will perceive the design and inherit the power to become 'joint-heirs with Christ.' Those who have freely elected not to listen will not perceive the design and will not inherit the power to become co-creative with God.

The human race will never fall into selfishness again. The meek shall inherit the Earth. The poor in spirit shall be enriched. Those who hunger after righteousness shall be fulfilled. And those who are attracted to the many mansions of the universe will explore the fascinating realms of inner and outer space beyond your present awareness.

# 4

# The Process Is
# Irreversible

*HEBREWS 6*

⁴ *For it is impossible for those who were once enlightened,
and have tasted of the heavenly gift, and were made partakers
of the Holy Ghost,*

⁵ *And have tasted the good word of God, and the powers of
the world to come,*

⁶ *If they shall fall away, to renew them again unto repen-
tance; seeing they crucify to themselves the Son of God
afresh, and put him to an open shame.*

Once you have committed yourself to evolution rather than
extinction, you set in motion an irreversible process. Once the
baby starts down the birth canal, it cannot return to the womb.
What one hour before was a safe home has become a lethal, suffo-
cating place.

Once you begin the process of self-evolution toward whole-
centeredness, you cannot return to the old limits of self-
centeredness. If you do, you will rip the fabric of your inner being
to shreds. You will suffocate your higher self, which has entered
into your system, turning on the mechanism of survival as a
Christ-like body and turning off the mechanism of survival as a
mammalian body.

The biological quantum instant for human beings occurs when the infant begins to breathe oxygen itself through the lungs. Once its umbilical cord is cut, it can no longer take oxygen directly from its mother.

The psychological quantum instant occurs when a person has passed from the womb of self-consciousness to the larger world of wholistic consciousness. This is the moment of 'rebirth,' or enlightenment. Once having experienced enlightenment you can no longer survive psychologically in the dark box of self-centeredness. That would be to the psyche what the return to the womb would be to the body.

There is yet another kind of quantum instant which is still to come. You have experienced the biological quantum instant at your birth. You experience the psychological quantum instant at your 'rebirth' of enlightenment and discovery of the Christ-within. You have yet to experience the planetary quantum instant, which is the forthcoming collective experience of oneness, universal life and shared contact with the God-force. In an instantaneous pentecost, a planetary smile will ripple through the minds of the self-elect upon the Earth, those who are choosing to transcend to the next stage of evolution, able now at last to transform their bodies from perishable to imperishable, to contact other life, to leave this Earth alive, and to know that they are natural Christs, universal humans, sons and daughters of God.

Once the planetary quantum instant has occurred, there will be an irreversible distinction between those who have chosen personal evolution and those who have chosen personal extinction.

Just as it is impossible for those who have been born biologically to return to the womb, it is impossible for those who have been reborn psychologically to return to the state of unknowing. Similarly, it will be impossible for those who are self-transformed within an interacting planetary system to return to the state of social separation.

Just as the cells are triggered into a new state by the birth of the baby, human beings will be triggered into a new state by the planetary birth experience. This event is as certain as the fact that once a child is conceived, it will surely be born. Even if it is aborted, it is *born* . . . dead. Even if it is still-born, it is *born* . . . dead. It must eject from the womb once it has been conceived.

And so it is with a planetary system. Once it has conceived self-conscious humans who learn the powers of science and technology through the development of their intellects, it *must* experience planetary oneness, birth and universal life.

Earth may be an abortive planet. It may be a still-born planet. It may be a healthy planet. In any case, you shall inevitably pass through this phase of evolution, never to go back again.

The process of evolution is irreversible, intentional and directional. An adult cannot become a child. A child cannot become an embryo. A planetary species—*Homo sapiens*—cannot return to the first Garden of Eden wherein the self separated out from animal consciousness. *Homo sapiens* can only go forward to the second Garden of Eden wherein resides the tree of life. You shall have the power of the gods and be godly—or you shall surely die. There is no other choice. Amen.

# 5
# Synergy

*MATTHEW 5*

[38] *Ye have heard that it hath been said, An eye for an eye, and a tooth for a tooth:*

[39] *But I say unto you, That ye resist not evil: but whosoever shall smite thee on thy right cheek, turn to him the other also.*

Herein lies the step from destruction to creation for planet Earth. If you do not obey this law, you will not be able to evolve. Even your Father in heaven cannot change this law because he created it as an eternal law, the immutable law of love.

Prior to the phase of conscious evolution, organisms evolve through a process of survival of the most cooperative clusters of molecules, cells, animals and humans. But the process is not self-conscious and one cooperative cluster often survives at the expense of another and, indeed, has to.

However, when you graduate from unconscious to conscious evolution, you begin to make visible the invisible hand of God. Individuals gain command of vast energies—nuclear forces, bio-engineering, satellites, rockets, lasers. At the same time, the world becomes increasingly interdependent, and the childish way of one group winning at the expense of others becomes destructive to winner and loser alike.

You can no longer play the I win/you lose game; that has become the *all*-lose game. Since all people are members of one body, everyone loses when society is structured in such a way that a 'winner' diminishes the rights of the loser.

Henceforth, only synergy will work. Synergy is the way to overcome your 'enemy' by including and incorporating him in the creation of a whole society that benefits him more than any partial victory of one over another. You must move beyond competition and co-existence to co-creation, as individuals, communities, nations and the world.

Synergy is pragmatic. It is the way nature works to create *more*—a profit for all—via a more integrated cooperation of the parts to form a whole society which is *more* than the sum of its parts. That 'more' is profit for each part.

"Love thy neighbor as thyself" is the pragmatic, ethical expression of how nature forms more complex, whole systems out of the dis-ordering of past systems. Those capable of following this great commandment even now find themselves participating in the formation of vital clusters of like-minded lovers. Energy is being given them.

People who attempt to maintain the old separatist stance, attempting to punish their enemies, will become increasingly removed from the growing edge of the human community. They will harden, calcify and eventually die of separation, no matter how long it takes.

Only love can achieve the next step of evolution. The separatists may impede the progress of those who love the world, but eventually they will change or else wither away through alienation, stress and discouragement. Love them, attract them, and leave them behind if they do not respond. Theirs is another day, another time, another cause.

Judge not that ye be not judged.

Create new ground for synergy where those attracted to building new worlds on Earth, new worlds in space, can work together without attacking anyone. There must be arenas where individuals are invited in and respond by their own free will.

Do not pour new wine into old bottles. Build new vehicles for synergistic action through which attracted individuals can create their hearts' desires. The new worlds can only be built by individuals co-creating freely, attracted by a transcendent possibility, rewarded by the acts of creation every step of the way, guided by an inner sense of the reality that all humans are members of one body and that the whole body is greater than and different from the sum of its parts.

It is a fact that whole systems differ from the sum of their parts. That accounts for newness. Synergy of separate parts creates the quantum transformation of new forms out of old.

At your stage of evolution, synergistic co-operation of human beings will create miracles. Wherever two or more agree upon anything, it shall surely be done, for such agreement implies that each member of that group has recognized neighbor as self.

This in-depth attunement brings in the power of the Creator. The creative power is attracted to centers of synergy. Such groups literally become infused with the creative ability of evolution and can transcend any obstacle they choose. Specifically, those who partake in synergistic clusters with the purpose of cooperating with the God-force to create new worlds on Earth and in space will find themselves being transformed personally. Even now, individuals are experiencing this change.

Here is the unexpected mystery, the unexpected reward, and the catalytic trigger to move millions of incipient conscious evolutionaries to action. There is the promise of personal transformation in your lifetime if you will partake of the full spectrum of human potential now available. You can begin your transformation now by practicing personal self-improvement, thought purification, body awareness, love of your neighbor as yourself, partaking of the benefits of the bio-medical advances in longevity, going into space, living and working beyond the biosphere, expanding your intelligence through positive thought, right aspiration and cybernetic extension.

You are the generation born when humankind is born. You are the first generation to be aware of yourself as one and responsible for the future of the whole. Your capacity as united humankind is infinitely greater than as individuals, separate and alone.

It's happening NOW. Your story is a birth—your own. What Christ came to Earth to demonstrate 2000 years ago as a single super-human, all can now begin as normal, fully-human beings, grateful for his affirmation of the potential which lies in each of you now.

# 6

# Love Conquers All

*MATTHEW 5*

⁴³ *Ye have heard that it hath been said, Thou shalt love thy neighbour, and hate thine enemy.*

⁴⁴ *But I say unto you, Love your enemies, bless them that curse you, do good to them that hate you, and pray for them which despitefully use you, and persecute you.*

The commandment is positive not negative. "Love your enemies" means do not fight negativity with its own weapons. Do not become negative in the attempt to defeat negation. To overcome 'evil,' become supremely positive, thereby converting it rather than succumbing to it by being forced to be destructive.

The method of converting evil—that which separates you from contact with God and your neighbor—is initiatory love. Initiatory love goes beyond passive love, which only responds to other love, "loving them which love you." Active love takes the initiative to love that which is not loving, but in fact *needs* love.

Initiatory love takes the position of Christ and is self-authorized, free and independent of the illusions of fear and separation which the 'enemy' might express. It recognizes all attack as expression of fear or a childish call for love. It responds, not with reaction, but with pro-action—loving strength, which both prevents destruction and attracts construction.

Initiatory love knows that the enemy is part of the same body. Initiatory love incorporates evil by refusing to react in fear. It reflects love in response to hate. In the mirror of that love, the hateful see a new image of themselves as lovable and become so.

There is no one on Earth who wants to be evil, and filled with hate. No one desires to be evil, even the worst criminal. It is fear that motivates acts of evil, fear and the illusion of separation—the forgetfulness that all people are members of one body.

You, my new world builders, must practice initiatory love. First, protect yourselves from the evil of acting destructively. Second, evolve yourselves into masters of co-creation wherein the power of your creativity is so dynamic that you convert the destroyers by the magnetism of your acts.

Among the miracles you are to perform is the conversion of the pessimists, the sorrowful and the sick of heart via the mass media. Convert them to joy, expectation, participation and anticipation of the new.

One such conversion on television—the 'mount' of this age—will reach the aching hearts of millions with the hope that the world is not dying, but being born. It will release the energy of hope in millions, revealing their pent-up power to them. Such a conversion can start the grain of mustard seed upon its cycle of growth. Once it has sprouted, if the soil is right and spring is near, nothing can stop its growth.

My beloved people of Earth, the time *is* right, the soil *is* ready, spring *is* near. Begin the conversion to hope by spreading the message of humanity's potentials to the members of the planetary body. Help them experience that the birth they are witnessing is their own.

# 7

# The Fruition of
# 2000 Years

*ACTS 13*

**38** *Be it known unto you therefore, men and brethren, that through this man is preached unto you the forgiveness of sins:*

**39** *And by him all that believe are justified from all things, from which ye could not be justified by the law of Moses.*

**40** *Beware therefore, lest that come upon you, which is spoken of in the prophets;*

**41** *Behold, ye despisers, and wonder, and perish: for I work a work in your days, a work which ye shall in no wise believe, though a man declare it unto you.*

How could the demonstration of one superhuman man save the rest of us from our sins? How could his capacity to transform his body from perishable to imperishable help us to do the same?

Here is an answer for those in the modern generation who have eyes to see and ears to hear: his demonstration can save us from death because he awakened in us the awareness that it is possible for us to do likewise. For he said we could do what he did—and more.

Once they were aware that this was possible, Jesus' followers set about to actualize the possibility. They stimulated our consciousness to expect something more than the mammalian life cycle, through love of God and each other. This awareness activated Western civilization by its affirmation of a personal existence beyond this life and in a new body.

It activated science and technology to probe the material world and discover how it works, lifting the veil of matter to penetrate the invisible processes of creation so we could transform our materiality.

It activated democratic institutions based on the sacredness of individuals as co-equal with and equally beloved by God. Democratic institutions liberated individual potential, which is bringing about the "end of the world" as we have known it, and the beginnings of new worlds as we co-create them in our growing knowledge of how God does it.

The awareness of our potential has already created capacities too great for Mother Earth to contain, thereby activating a planetary meta-crisis of limitation and over-complexity which cannot be managed by science and democracy alone. The powers that led us to the meta-crisis are insufficient to overcome it. The meta-crisis created by science and democracy is forcing us to fuse the human intellect with spiritual intuition and to discover the evolutionary design as a guide for change.

What is the evolutionary design? It is the expression of spirit. It is not material, but rather the intention which directs universal energy.

Jesus best demonstrated the evolutionary design, which the intuition is now pressured to reveal as the intellect falters in the face of planetary crises beyond its capacity to model or to manage.

Jesus demonstrated the recurring pattern in billions of years of growth history: when life hits a crisis of limitations, it innovates and transforms by creating new, more complex bodies capable of increased consciousness, freedom and order. This is what Jesus did. He took the next quantum leap—in one lifetime—from animal human to universal human by creating a new "glorified body" which could transcend the terrestrial-physical frontier.

He has 'saved' us by giving us, via his demonstration, the awareness, encouragement, expectation and permission that it is right and possible for human beings to transcend their animal inheritance.

It is the animal (mortal) body that holds us to an illusion of separation, and it is the sense of separation that gives rise to sin. As we overcome the mortal body, we overcome the sin of separation and rejoin the creation as imperishable children of God—at the beginning of the next phase of life.

Because Paul thought the end of the world was at hand in his lifetime, he urged people to repent, believe and be prepared for the second coming, when the dead would be raised incorruptible and the disbelievers would become extinct.

He did not expect that a church would have to endure almost two thousand years, preserving the seed, keeping the flame of expectation alive through the cruel darkness of self-centered infant human history.

There are those among us who feel now, as Paul did then, that the hour of the second coming is at hand. Why do we believe this is true, when for almost two thousand years life has proceeded, incremental step by incremental step? We believe the second coming, or the quantum transformation, is at hand because incremental steps no longer are adequate. We have reached the threshold of a whole-system change.

For the first time we recognize the limits to growth on a finite planet. For the first time we can terminate all human life on this planet by destroying its biosphere. We cannot continue to grow as before, nor can we continue to resolve our conflicts by violent means, because the power to destroy has escalated to overkill. To continue as before would lead to self-destruction.

The alternative lies in other 'firsts.' For the first time we can leave this earth alive. For the first time we can change the design of our bodies. For the first time we can create new bodies by conscious conception. For the first time we can create intelligent bodies in our cybernetic instruments. For the first time we can probe the workings of the nervous system and brain.

Our unprecedented powers of destruction and our unprecedented powers of co-creation are forcing us and attracting us into a quantum change, a radical leap from the root of our potential into the next phase of our being. We cannot continue as we have for the past two thousand years and survive. We are a child in the womb who is overdue. Further growth, further exercise of capacity on this plane, within the confines of this environment, will destroy our opportunity.

The hour of transformation is at hand. The process has begun, of which Paul preached and for which the millions of souls during the culmination of Earth-bound history have prayed. The prayers of two thousand years are mingling with the scientific genius of the human race, to propel us through the meta-crises to the meta-opportunities of the first phase of universal consciousness and action.

How long will the process of transformation last? How long is the great transition? What is the timing of planetary birth? It is quick! "In the twinkling of an eye," wrote Paul, all shall be changed. The sufferings of the present will be forgotten in the glory which shall be revealed. The former things will pass away, and will scarcely be remembered; just as we cannot remember our life in the womb of our mother, so we will be unable to remember our life in the womb-phase of terrestrial life.

The transition will accelerate in the next generation—twenty to fifty years can reveal the outline of universal humanity, if we so choose. We have free will. The choice is ours. We cannot choose whether or not the world will transform. We can only choose whether the process will be graceful or disastrous.

All the problems accelerate exponentially in the next twenty years; over-population, pollution, depletion of non-renewable resources, arms escalation and self-centered conflict cannot continue in a closed system. They *will* be stopped, either willingly by choice or forcibly by natural catastrophe.

All the potentials also accelerate exponentially in the next twenty years—if we choose to fulfill them. Nature will not do this automatically. The potentials can only be fulfilled by conscious and collective willingness to do. Human settlement of outer space, longevity, increased intelligence, and other potentials, if actualized, will interact synergistically upon each other, creating a quantum leap in human performance in one generation.

We are now in a sorting-out phase. Those who elect to transform are being magnetized by their attraction to the next phase. Those who do not elect to transform are being turned off by their repulsion to the next phase. By attraction and repulsion the selection is being made.

Within one generation the first child will be born in outer space beyond the womb of Earth, beyond the static of a biosphere which still rings with the cries of terror and pain of all the creatures who kill and are killed on Earth. This child will look outward to Earth as a world it has never seen, a way of life it has never known. It will live in an environment consciously designed by human intelligence in cooperation with the laws of nature and the intention of creation. It will hear of the tales of its terrestrial origins with amazement. It will ask: "How could it be that we could go so long without knowing we are all part of the same creation, imbued with the power of the Creator, working in cooperation with all life?"

The first generation to be conceived in space will have a slightly different genetic code. The step towards imperishable bodies will be made. The era of natural Christs will begin. The root of human evil will be exorcised forever.

David saw corruption; his body was mortal. Jesus saw incorruption; he built a new body. The root of human evil is the corruptibility of the body. The mortality of the body causes fear everlasting.

Our animal origins are imprinted on that body. Out of the darkness of kill and be killed, where millions of species eat each other alive—out of this environment of violence we have risen. Our sensitive nervous systems carry the memory of pain immemorial. In the terror that flesh and blood will perish is one of the roots of human evil.

> *And God said, Behold, I have given you every herb bearing seed, which is upon the face of all the earth, and every tree, in which is the fruit of a tree yielding seed; to you it shall be for meat.*
>
> *And to every beast of the earth, and to every fowl of the air, and to every thing that creepeth upon the earth, wherein there is life, I have given every green herb for meat: and it was so. (Genesis 1:29,30)*

Unfortunately, it was not so. Although the design revealed in Genesis prohibits killing to eat, killing became 'natural.' Multicellular organisms committed the 'sin' of self-consumption and passed the trait of the taste of flesh on to us.

Cain and Abel are the first *human* instance of killing, but not the first killing on Earth. The remarkable fact of the story of Cain and Abel was the awareness that we should *not* kill; that was *new* with the human race.

We have been struggling up out of the animal condition of kill and be killed. The sense of guilt awoke with the dawn of self-consciousness. We separated out from the animal world, yet saw ourselves behaving as animals—and were revolted. We tried to transcend ourselves, to be "perfect as our Father in Heaven is perfect." But we still had the animal bodies. Our bodies hungered and thirsted, desired and conquered, killed and were killed, lusted and possessed.

Nevertheless, something in us would not totally accommodate to the animal behavior. We struggled to overcome it. With passion we tried to pacify ourselves and live at peace on Earth. In so doing we occasionally behaved even worse than animals. The intellect, mingling with animal emotions, created horrendous crimes against life—tortures, wars, incarcerations, inquisitions, deaths by the millions. Oh humanity, how painful is our terrestrial past!

Now, at last, we are on the verge of transcending the limits of the animal condition by changing our bodies from perishable to imperishable, leaving this Earth alive, and aligning our wills with the will of the Creator. We are on the verge of doing what Jesus did through the harmonious use of the collective capacities of the whole planetary body politic.

We will not transcend to the next phase of evolution as individuals, separate and alone. For collective salvation we need the collective capacities of humankind. Thus the next step of evolution is not the ascension of individuals after death, leaving the corruptible body to return to dust. The next step of evolution is the transformation of individuals through changing the body, as Jesus demonstrated, leaving no remains on Earth.

We shall be free of the mortal condition. It was an evolutionary phase, like single-celled life. When the phase passes, we shall be free to face the next set of challenges, the next emancipation of potential, until the universe is alive with consciousness that we are at one with God, inheritors of the whole Creation.

# 8

# Will You Be at the Party?

*TITUS 1*

¹⁰ *For there are many unruly and vain talkers and deceivers, specially they of the circumcision:*

¹¹ *Whose mouths must be stopped, who subvert whole houses, teaching things which they ought not, for filthy lucre's sake . . . .*

¹³ *This witness is true. Wherefore rebuke them sharply, that they may be sound in the faith.*

The time for "rebuke" is over. The selection process that separates the wheat from the chaff, the sheep from the goats, the self-elected from the self-rejected is not of human origin. We are not the judge of one another. We are not the jury. We merely choose for ourselves.

The selection process has been in operation since the universe began. It is the whole-making mechanism that selects those particles capable of uniting with other particles, thus making whole systems greater than the sum of their parts. We are selected for our capacity to synergize, to become whole enough to enter into larger, more complex wholes, to carry out the intentionality of the evolutionary process to attain ever greater freedom, consciousness and union with the God force.

The evolutionary selection process is God in the role of editor of his own creation. We no longer need accept the responsibility which Paul undertook in "stopping the mouths of the unruly talkers and deceivers." Although they are still in our midst, we are not responsible for their behavior. This is because we are now entering the period of the quantum instant. The pressure of God's selection mechanism is intensifying. Those who are self-rejecting, choosing not to fulfill their own potential, not to nurture the growth of the natural Christ within, are under sufficient pressure from the whole system. The system's 'vengeance' is sufficient to alert them to their condition. God does not need our help in alerting people to their faults.

The selection process is signaling each of us by means of pain and stress. Whenever one of us feels distressed, it is a signal that we are not nurturing the Christ within. The stress signal is an evolutionary helper alerting us to re-align, to pacify our egos, to calm our childish emotions, to remember we are the heirs of God.

We need not rebuke each other for forgetting. We can help each other remember. We can best help others by helping ourselves and thereby demonstrating the state of being of a natural Christ. That state is so attractive, so joyful, that it gives people a positive shock, a charge of energy to activate their own evolutionary potential.

If others do not respond to their own inner growth, they are not meant to evolve—that is the impersonal justice in the whole system. If you do not *choose* to evolve, you do not evolve. It is up to you. No one can choose for you. Nor can anyone deny you the choice. Freedom is inherent in the nature of reality.

# 9

# Going the Whole Way

*LUKE 9*

⁵¹ *And it came to pass, when the time was come that he should be received up, he stedfastly set his face to go to Jerusalem.*

There comes a time in each of your lives when you must steadfastly set your face "to go to Jerusalem." If you do so, you transcend your limits. If you do not, you submit to your limits.

The decision to go to Jerusalem is the inner choice to "pay all for all," to give your uttermost to what you believe is the highest good.

Everyone has that choice. In this choice, everyone is equal. No matter what your external condition, rich or poor, sick or well, you can choose to go the whole way, or to stop somewhere below the peak of your vision.

There are no excuses. There is no one to blame if you choose not to go. No one can make a victim out of you. No circumstance, no deprivation, no ignominy, no pain can render you a victim if you choose to be a co-creator and set your face to go to Jerusalem.

This truth is profoundly liberating. You know that *you* are in charge of your own transcendence.

\* \* \*

Jesus' life is a sublime example of human power to choose not to be a victim. He specifically accepted humanness to demonstrate that human power can overcome its own limits when this power is freely and fully aligned with God's.

That is the essence of his capacity to save us. He revealed to us that each of us can choose to transform himself or herself by following his way—that is, by loving God above all else and our neighbor as ourself. That he "died to save us" means that he demonstrated once and for all that our potential is not to submit to death but to transform ourselves into a new being.

Just as we are the cause, not the effect of our lives, we are the cause, not the effect of our material expression. We can heal our sickness. We can stimulate our self-healing powers by recognizing ourselves as already perfect, whole, the cause of our own lives with our source connected to the creative source of the universe, to God.

We can restore the Earth by recognizing it as our large body and healing it by the same re-cognition with which we heal ourselves. We can transcend the Earth by recognizing that the existing planetary body is not our limit any more than the existing physical body is. We can transcend by the use of our total power and authority in alignment with the designing intelligence.

Jerusalem no longer means sacrifice, crucifixion and death. It means resurrection, transformation and life everlasting.

It takes only one example to show that something is possible. One landing on the moon is all that was necessary to demonstrate that we are not Earthbound. One resurrection is all that was needed to demonstrate the possibility of life everlasting in new bodies.

# 10

# The Inner Telephone

*HEBREWS 2*

[16] *For verily he took not on him the nature of angels; but he took on him the seed of Abraham.*

[17] *Wherefore in all things it behoved him to be made like unto his brethren, that he might be a merciful and faithful high priest in things pertaining to God, to make reconciliation for the sins of the people.*

[18] *For in that he himself hath suffered being tempted, he is able to succour them that are tempted.*

You have assistance, dearly beloveds. You have help. Jesus Christ is still a living consciousness. He experienced the full cup of human joy and suffering in a body like yours in order to demonstrate to you that you can do as he did and more. He is ready to help you now if you choose to evolve.

How can he who is so far above help you who is so close to the ground? Can't a parent help a child? Can't an older brother help a younger? Can't a teacher help a student?

Thus can the Christ help you. When you call on his "succour" two things happen. First of all you activate your own Christ-abilities. Just as your autonomic nervous system pumps adrenalin into your body to give you extra strength when you are in danger, so you pump co-creative energy into your system when you call upon the Christ. He is the opposite of the idea of danger. He is the idea of security, salvation, eternal life. This idea floods your system with impulses that signal all your cells and organs to perform in synchronicity, harmony and tranquility. This in turn starts the self-healing and self-regenerating mechanism that strengthens and transforms you into his likeness—which is you at your next stage of evolution.

The second way he helps is that by your call to him you are actually signaling a responsive consciousness that is omnipresent in the universe. It is literally like calling a friend on the phone.

Would you have guessed you could make a phone call before the phone was invented? Can you imagine how strange it sounded to your fathers when they first picked up the phone and called across the valley to another? They used to shout! But you know that it is not necessary to shout. Your voice is carried by invisible vibrations that register upon the ear of the listener, wherein it sets up sympathetic action impinging on the brain, which translates vibrations to meaning—all without you knowing how it is done. A two-year-old child could do it, once Alexander Graham Bell invented the phone.

Bell discovered how the process of sound works and built an instrument to work with it. You have an instrument within you, as reliable as the phone, which most people have not yet learned to use, the instrument of directed thought, or telepathy. You have a telepathic 'telephone' in your mind which can call upon any consciousness that ever lived by the simple process of focused thought.

The reason you do not do this well is that you have not learned to concentrate your thought. You are always attending to extraneous ideas, hidden fears, guilt, wayward thoughts. You have not learned to build the inner sound studio to be inaccessible to negative thoughts. It is this 'static' in your receiving and sending apparatus that prevents you from using your innate telepathic capacity to call upon the Christ—or anyone else.

The universe is sensitive to thought. Practice thinking exactly what you want to think and nothing else. Focus, focus, focus. Let the magnetic needle of your attention point to the highest signal you can hear—and send forth upon that inner communication system a call for assistance whenever you so desire. Ask and it shall be answered. Try and you shall see. You shall see.

# 11

# Focus

*I PETER 1*

*3 Blessed be the God and Father of our Lord Jesus Christ, which according to his abundant mercy hath begotten us again unto a lively hope by the resurrection of Jesus Christ from the dead,*

*4 To an inheritance incorruptible, and undefiled, and that fadeth not away, reserved in heaven for you,*

*5 Who are kept by the power of God through faith unto salvation ready to be revealed in the last time . . . .*

*13 Wherefore gird up the loins of your mind, be sober, and hope to the end for the grace that is to be brought unto you at the revelation of Jesus Christ.*

Focus, focus, focus your attention on your goal.

Your goal is to become a natural Christ. This is the incorruptible inheritance reserved for you by the power of God through your faith, until it will be revealed in the "last time," in the quantum instant, when the New Order of the Ages shall be apparent and the old order shall be in obvious disarray.

Your faith and your focus upon this goal is essential to your achieving your inheritance. It cannot be given to you if you are a passive or negligent creature going about your selfish business with no interest in what you are to become.

A parent cannot give a child its inheritance until the child has matured enough to know its value. You cannot receive your inheritance—the full powers of a co-creator—until you have matured enough to know its value and are prepared to use the powers with responsibility.

The key now is where you place your attention. Place your attention on the image of yourself as a natural Christ. Perform the cosmic union ceremony, the next and universal stage of the communion service that has been practiced faithfully for two thousand years in preparation for my second coming:

Visualize a cocoon of light. Within this cocoon visualize the body of Jesus the Christ, glowing with light. He is in the cave, rebuilding his body. Step into the cave. Penetrate the cocoon. Enter your body into his body of light. Let the light enlighten your body until it vibrates at the same frequency as his.

Call to him:

> I am a body of light,
> you are a body of light.
> Fuse your light with mine
> so that I may be charged
> with the electricity of your being,
> so that I will be changed
> to become like you.
> I ask my body to change
> from perishable to imperishable.
> It knows how.
> It awaits my conscious decision
> to transform.

Call for the Holy Spirit:

> Brighten the cocoon of light.
> Nothing can penetrate
> this membrane of light.

I call for the Holy Spirit,
God's communication system,
to infuse my being,
to be with me all day,
guiding my every action,
guarding my every thought,
giving me the comfort I need
to act out of love, not lack.

Energize me with
the fire of love,
the light of wisdom,
the electricity of attraction,
the magnetism of will,
oriented to the purpose of my life
which is
to become
a natural Christ,
an heir of God.

Guard me from separation this day
that thy will, and mine
which now are one,
shall be done.
Amen.

# 12

# Becoming Natural Christs

*COLOSSIANS 3*

*¹ If ye then be risen with Christ, seek those things which are above, where Christ sitteth on the right hand of God.*

*² Set your affection on things above, not on things on the earth . . . .*

*⁵ Mortify therefore your members which are upon the earth; fornication, uncleanness, inordinate affection, evil concupiscence, and covetousness, which is idolatry . . .*

*⁸ But now ye also put off all these; anger, wrath, malice, blasphemy, filthy communication out of your mouth.*

*⁹ Lie not one to another, seeing that ye have put off the old man with his deeds;*

*¹⁰ And have put on the new man, which is renewed in knowledge after the image of him that created him:*

*¹¹ Where there is neither Greek nor Jew, circumcision nor uncircumcision, Barbarian, Scythian, bond nor free: but Christ is all, and in all.*

Those of you who wish to become natural Christs must do as he did in every thought, word and deed. You must recognize that you are responsible for everything you think and do.

You will begin to evolve yourself from self-centered fear to whole-centered love. Every time you catch yourself forgetting who you are becoming, you may remind yourself instantaneously, and re-imagine yourself as a son or daughter of God, an heir to the kingdom, a joint heir with Christ, a universal co-creator.

Every time you shift your thought from self to whole you create a spiritual reflex action—a "habit of elevation" which will begin to be second nature. Your first nature will fade away. Your second nature will unfold until you always, naturally, spontaneously think, act and experience as did Jesus—your higher self.

This spiritual training is of immeasurable value. The pathways of perception, once established, will trigger a co-creative nature within you as demonstrably different from your present nature as puberty and the activated reproduction system is from childhood. "You shall not all sleep, you shall all be changed." This is the first step of the change. Set your affection on things above.

You do not need to "mortify your members" as Paul suggested two thousand years ago. You need only to give your members—the various aspects of your personality—total forgiveness, total unconditional love. Do as Jesus did: forgive the 'sinners' within you and put your attention in yourself as Christ.

Sin is the illusion of separation. You could not possibly do any of those 'evil' acts in a state of wholistic consciousness wherein you remember you are one with all being.

Fornication, uncleanness, inordinate affection, evil concupiscence, covetousness, anger, wrath, malice, blasphemy, filthy communication, lies—all are impossible if you know you are an heir apparent to the invisible processes of creation, beloved by the Creator of the universe, needed for the evolution of the world.

Do not spend your energy focusing on your faults. Pay attention to your virtues. Lift your sights to your highest intentions and do only that always. Your sins will disappear. They were only the result of the illusion that you, the creature, were separate from the Creator. You are not.

The Christian Church suffered deeply from Paul's words: "mortify therefore your members which are upon the earth." His anger at the "vile body," his pronouncements against sin are un-Christlike. Jesus said, "you are forgiven; go, sin no more." He never asked sinners to focus on their weakness. He asked them instead to have absolute faith in God.

Paul, being human, fell into the fateful trap of anger against human limitations. Such anger strengthens those limits. The Christian world developed a focus on the evil of the flesh, which condemned the world to centuries of *self*-condemnation. From Augustine to St. Francis—800 years—the ideal of the Christian world was mortification of the flesh.

Francis reinstated Jesus' ideal of pure love. He noticed that God created the heavens and the earth. He extended love to all the created creatures—the birds, the animals, the trees. However, he stopped at the threshold of his own body. He became angry at it, for it desired comfort. He abused his body to the point of death.

All of this happened because the end did not come, the tribulations did not begin, the time of the transformation was not yet at hand. Paul, Augustine, Francis and the rest were burdened with the awful task of preserving the seed of hope for a new body through the cold, slow winter of incremental change—until now, when the rains are falling, the sun is rising, the waters are warming, the seeds are sprouting.

You are born in the spring. You no longer need to condemn the old mammalian body for keeping you from becoming imperishable. You can focus all your energy on the actual task of becoming imperishable. What does this mean? It means:

- Purify your thoughts. Think only those thoughts you think with Christ.
- Purify your body. Release it from stress. Give it pure food. Do not abuse it with excess. Exercise it gently, and ask it to evolve. Tell your cellular intelligence you are ready to become a natural Christ, doing your Father's work on Earth as it is in heaven. The intention is a signal to the hormonal system.
- Pray incessantly to know the Creator's will, so you can join your will to his. Create the still place to listen to the voice for God.
- Recognize at all times that everybody is the child of God. Substitute love for fear, forgiveness for condemnation.
- Support scientific research into the genetic intelligence so that you can learn the language of the genes. The key to body transformation is a combination of inner attraction to becoming your potential self, and external knowledge of

genetic language, plus another factor: your entry into outer space.

- Get yourself a ticket to outer space. Support the space program so that you can let your body experience the new environment beyond the womb of Earth. The new body will not be activated until the new cosmic environment is accessible. Imperishable beings do not belong in a finite biosphere. The process cannot fulfill itself so long as we are Earthbound.

"If ye then be risen with Christ, seek those things which are above, where Christ sitteth on the right hand of God."

"Above" has a two-fold meaning. On the inner plane it means seeking to become a natural Christ, a fully-realized human. On the external plane it means leaving this Earth alive and experiencing yourself as independent from your terrestrial body. The external plane is a *new* opportunity upon which the whole creation waited. It is part of the mystery which could not be told, because it would have seemed impossible to a pre-scientific world.

But now you know, dearly beloveds. Act upon what you know. *Thy* will be done on Earth as it is in heaven, for thy will and thy Father's will are one. That is the faith of the Father to the son.

# 13

# Reveal the Glory

Dearly beloveds—you who are answering the call of your higher self to be like me, to be natural Christs—all praise to you.

I thank you, brother and sister humans, for your faith in me, during the terrible sufferings which you have undergone. I know how it feels, for I have felt it. I also know how it feels to overcome it. And so shall you.

You are entering the home stretch, O people of God. Do not waver now.

Now is the time
when the people of God
must demonstrate what it means
to be godly.

You must reveal the glory
which is me in you
by acting up to your highest potential,
right now,
for all to see.

This means:
Do not give in to any fear.
Love God above all else,
love your neighbor as yourself,
and allow your body-mind to transform.
Your body wants to regenerate,
to become like mine.
Let it do so.
Your mind wants to attune to God,
to become like mine.
Let it do so.

Your role now, dearly beloved people of God,
is to demonstrate Christ-capacities.
Heal!
Rejuvenate!
Love!
Attune!
Ascend!

Empower all you meet to do the same.

Thank you.
Amen.

# A New Heaven
# and a New Earth

*(What follows is the first entry in the manuscript titled,* The Book of Co-Creation: An Evolutionary Interpretation of the New Testament. *It is repeated here just as it came to me. —BMH)*

*MATTHEW 1*

¹*The book of the generation of Jesus Christ, the son of David, the son of Abraham.*

The generation of Jesus Christ began with Abraham and reaches its conclusion in you who are born at the end of this phase of evolution, at the beginning of the new.

Abraham was the first human on planet Earth to demonstrate in his life the truth that there is One God, the Creator of the whole Creation, who is in partnership with His creature humanity who is to co-create with Him a new Heaven and a new Earth. This is the promised land. This is the covenant. This is the truth which shall be revealed.

Abraham kept that covenant. He began the demonstration that God and humanity are in partnership for the transformation of the world. Together they shall co-create the new Jerusalem, where there shall be no more death, neither sorrow, nor crying, neither shall there be any more pain: for the former things are passed away. We have been strangers in this holy city. We shall be strangers no more.

This is the covenant between Abraham and God that I, Jesus Christ, came to fulfill through my demonstration of the crucifixion, the resurrection, the ascension, and the promise that he who believes in me, the works that I do shall he do also, and greater works that these shall he do.

Everyone who believes in me may have life everlasting. I will raise him up at the last day.

You, dearly beloveds, are born on the last day. You are the generation born when humankind is born from Earth-only to universal life.

You now know you are one body into this universe seeking greater awareness of your creative intention, which is to become like me, a natural Christ, a co-creator of a new Heaven and a new Earth wherein the world will be restored, the people will be free, and you shall set forth to bring new life from Earth into the universe without end.

My birth, death, resurrection and ascension established the first demonstration of the future human. I am the template of what you potentially are.

My body and spirit are the temple which you shall also build. Your generation is the one to demonstrate the reality of human potential to become a natural Christ, a full human. Your generation is the first to have the power to transform your bodies and to ascend from this Earth in chariots of flaming fire.

You are the inheritors of the powers of creation. Through the maturation of intellect and individuality, you have discovered the invisible technologies of God's process of change. Into your hands, dearly beloveds, have been placed the understanding of the atom, the gene, the brain. Into your hands have been placed the power to build new worlds on Earth and in space. Into your hands have been given the authority to begin the building of the new Jerusalem which is the goal of human history.

The new Jerusalem is the next stage of evolution. It will be a community of natural Christs, cooperating with each other and God, endowed with the capacity to overcome hunger, death, planet-boundedness and separation from the universal community of life in the many mansions of this infinite world.

This is written for the co-creators of new worlds, the builders of a new Heaven and a new Earth. It is written for those now on Earth in whom the flame of expectation burns. It is written for those who wish to become like me, to do as I did and even more. It is written to the generation born in the fullness of time. When the transformation has come, the selection must be made, the choice for life ever-evolving is open at last.

This is a moment of cosmic choice for the peoples of Earth. You have been given the power to build new worlds, or to destroy your world. You stand at the brink of Armageddon.

You see beyond you the new Jerusalem—the vision of yourselves in the future which I come to Earth to reveal. You see the abyss between here and there. In the *Book of Revelation*, John described the violent path to the new Jerusalem; it is the way for a planet whose people refuse to give up their selfish life.

In this text we will discover a loving path to the new Jerusalem. It is a path for a planet whose people choose to use their power, in all its splendor, for the transformation of the whole body.

The choice is given to your generation. There are alternatives to the tribulations. There are graceful births toward universal life based on the reality of your potentials. This text is a description of the truth of my life in the light of what you have learned through intellect and individuality, through science and democracy, since I came to Earth nearly two thousand years ago.

*Evolution proceeds by choice
not by chance
from this stage onward.*